Finlay and Julia Graham:
Missionary Partners
JOHNNIE HUMAN
Illustrated by Ron Hester

BROADMAN PRESS
Nashville, Tennessee

4243-27
ISBN: 0-8054-4327-4

Dewey Decimal Classification: J266.092
Subject Headings:
GRAHAM, FINLAY / / GRAHAM, JULIA / / MISSIONS—MIDDLE EAST

Library of Congress Catalog Card Number: 86-4148
Printed in the United States of America

Library of Congress Cataloging-in-Publication Data

Human, Johnnie.
Finlay and Julia Graham: missionary partners.

Summary: Describes the work of Finlay and Julia
Graham, missionaries in the Middle East, discussing
the events leading up to their call to missions.
   1. Graham, Finlay—Juvenile literature. 2. Graham,
Julia—Juvenile literature. 3. Missionaries—Near
East—Biography—Juvenile literature. 4. Missionaries—
United States—Biography—Juvenile literature.
5. Southern Baptist Convention—Missions—Near East—
Juvenile literature. [1. Graham, Finlay. 2. Graham,
Julia. 3. Missionaries] I. Hester, Ronald, ill.
II. Title.
BV3202.G73H86   1986   266'.6132'0922 [B] [920] 86-4148
ISBN 0-8054-4327-4

Dedicated to
Karen Weatherford
Ann McClard
Connie White
Carolyn Ingram
who, through all my years of writing for children, have demonstrated their Christian patience and love by deciphering my handwriting and typing my manuscripts. My writing is actually a joint ministry with each of these, for without their commitment, my writing would have been more difficult and, at times, impossible.

Contents

A Lonely Train Ride

"Come quickly," Mrs. Saccar said anxiously to her husband on the phone. "And bring the doctor! I think I have found what's wrong with Julia. Hurry!"

The excitement in her voice caused Mr. Saccar and the doctor to run from the drugstore to the Saccar home. They didn't stop to ask questions. Something must have happened to Julia, the Saccars' only child.

Mrs. Saccar told the doctor Julia had had the worst coughing spell ever. The mother had placed her finger inside the baby's throat to help her cough up what was causing the problem. Mrs. Saccar felt something hard lodged in the baby's throat.

The doctor examined the sixteen-month-old baby carefully, just as he had done several times before. The baby had the worst case of whooping cough he had ever seen. The doctor had tried all remedies he knew. And Mrs. Saccar had tried a few others her neighbors and friends had suggested.

But Julia became worse every day. She grew weaker and weaker.

"I am sorry, Mrs. Saccar," the doctor said patiently. "But there is nothing in Julia's throat."

"I know I felt something," Mrs. Saccar insisted. Her husband and the doctor tried to comfort her. But she kept saying she was right. Only an X ray could tell whether something really was in Julia's throat.

But there were no X-ray machines in Hallettsville, Texas, in 1918. The closest one was in a hospital in Cuero, almost fifty miles away.

"I must take her. I know what I felt," Mrs. Saccar kept repeating.

"I'll borrow my mother's car and take you," Mr. Saccar said. He went to talk to his mother.

"Nonsense," Julia's grandmother said. "If the doctor says nothing is in Julia's throat, why take her on such a trip?" she asked. "You cannot take my car."

"Then I'll take her by train," Mrs. Saccar said.

Mr. Saccar took his determined wife and desperately sick baby to the train station. He did not believe the baby had anything in her throat. But his wife was sure she did. And he wanted so much for his baby to get well!

The train ride took several hours. As the minutes crept by, Mrs. Saccar began to wonder whether she was right. Then she looked down at her only child, Julia. She had to do everything possible to save her baby. Julia could no longer eat or swallow. "How much longer can she live like this?" her mother wondered.

Very late at night Mrs. Saccar and Julia arrived in Cuero and went straight to the hospital emergency room.

The X ray showed a six-penny nail lodged in the baby's throat. The doctor immediately performed surgery to remove it.

During the operation, a storm left the hospital without electricity. The doctor completed the surgery by lamplight. To this day, Julia has a two-inch scar on her neck from that operation.

"The baby could not have lived twenty-four more hours without the surgery," the doctor told Mrs. Saccar. "She would have died of gangrene because the nail was already getting rusty. Or, the nail would have punctured her lung, and people would have thought she died of tuberculosis, a serious lung disease," he said.

After the nail was found, the mother figured out what must have happened. Several weeks earlier, carpenters had been at their house enlarging the back porch. Before Mrs. Saccar knew it, Julia toddled to the new porch from the room where her mother was sewing.

Suddenly Julia coughed. Mrs. Saccar ran to her and pulled several tacks from her mouth. Julia must have swallowed the nail before she put the tacks in her mouth.

She did not have whooping cough at all.

Not long after that, the Saccars moved to San Antonio. The first Sunday they were there, Mrs. Saccar joined First Baptist Church. She and Julia attended all the services there—Sunday School, Training Union, the women's missionary meetings, and worship services.

Mr. Saccar belonged to a church of another denomination, but he rarely went to church. He was a pharmacist and worked long hours in his drugstore. He had little interest in church activities.

Julia went everywhere with her mother. When she was older, Julia often read the program parts when someone was absent. She learned about missions before she could even pronounce the names of people and places.

Two Big Decisions

One day in Sunday School, Mrs. Haycraft, the teacher, talked with the children about giving their lives to Christ. Julia really wanted to become a Christian. She told her teacher she wanted to make Jesus her Lord and Savior.

Happily, Julia told her mother about her decision. She wanted to be baptized. Her mother told her she must wait until she was older. Her mother wanted Julia to be sure she understood exactly what becoming a Christian meant.

Julia went to church every time she could. When she was ten years old, she attended a Training Union study course. Her group studied *Trailblazers in Other Lands*, a book about missionaries. Mrs. Brock taught Julia's group.

On Wednesday evening, Mrs. Brock told about David Livingstone, a foreign missionary in Africa. As Julia listened to the story of this brave missionary, she felt God was calling her to be a foreign missionary.

Julia told no one of her decision, not even her teacher or her mother. But she felt happy that she was going to do something special for God.

"Julia, I want to talk to you about something," her mother said one day. "You have become a Christian and want to be baptized. But your grandmother would really like for you to belong to a church of your father's denomination. I would like for you to go to church with your dad one Sunday and with me the next Sunday. I want you to be sure of what you believe before you are baptized. Will you do that?"

"Of course, I'll go, Mother, if that is what you want. But I'll miss being with my friends at church every Sunday morning," Julia replied.

For almost a year, Julia went with her father every other Sunday. Each Sunday she went she disliked going to her father's church a little more.

"Mother, I really like the Baptist church," she finally told her mother. "I do not like going to the other church at all. Must I keep going?"

Her mother agreed she could go only to the Baptist church.

Julia felt that her father was as relieved as she, since he did not want to go to church at all.

One Sunday morning, when Julia was twelve years old, Dr. I. E. Gates was preaching. During the invitation, Julia felt she must go forward and tell Dr. Gates she wanted to be baptized because she was already a Christian.

"No matter what anyone said, I had to go forward today," she explained to her mother.

"I am so happy for you, Julia," her mother said. "I wanted you to go forward in church when you had that kind of feeling. I know you are a Christian. Now you can be baptized and join the church."

That very night, the pastor baptized Julia.

Julia liked going to school, but she hated playing games outdoors. She dreaded the day each year when soft-ball season began.

"It's time to go outside to play softball," her schoolteacher said. "Joan and Mary will be captains and will choose their teams."

As usual, Mary chose Julia last, after everyone else was selected. No team ever wanted Julia. And she didn't blame the others. When she pitched the ball, even she couldn't tell where the ball would go. And everyone clapped when Julia hit the ball with a bat. Most of the time she missed.

Julia could not play volleyball either.

"Julia, have you ever served that ball over the net?" a friend asked one day.

"Not that I can remember," Julia answered. "Some of us have no talent for playing any kind of ball."

Julia did not care for piano lessons, either, though she took two lessons a week.

"You must practice," her mother said. "Practice a half hour every morning and a half hour every afternoon."

Julia set a clock on the piano. She knew she had to practice thirty minutes, but not a second longer. As soon as the half hour was up, she stopped playing. She refused to play even one note after the time was up.

Later, as a missionary, Julia was glad she had learned to play the piano. She could read music so well that she could play any piece of music given to her.

One thing Julia did like was acting. She was in her first play during kindergarten. She liked acting so much that she knew she had found a special talent.

Many of her friends took expression lessons to learn how to speak and to act in dramatic plays. Julia finally convinced her mother to let her take two expression lessons each week and give up the piano lessons.

Julia invited her friends home with her often. No matter how many she brought, Mrs. Saccar was glad to see them. And jars of chocolate, sugar, and oatmeal cookies always lined the shelf, just waiting for each girl to choose the kind she liked best.

A Friend Named Henry

One day at church, Julia met a new family, the Hagoods. Their son, Henry, was the same age as Julia. Henry and Julia soon became friends. Henry also felt God wanted him to be a foreign missionary.

When Henry and Julia were fifteen, they began dating. One day they talked about how they felt about each other. They were happy that God had called them both to be foreign missionaries. Henry told Julia he wanted her to marry him.

Since they were only fifteen, Julia's mother did not think it was a serious romance. "You will fall in and out of love many times before you marry," her mother told Julia. But Julia and Henry knew their love would last.

When they were seventeen, Sunday School leaders asked them to teach thirteen-year-olds. Julia taught the girls. Henry taught the boys. Both of them had fun teaching and planning parties for their classes.

Julia kept taking her expression lessons. One day Mrs. Matthews, her teacher, had exciting news to tell Julia.

"A talent scout from Hollywood wants to come here to meet you," Mrs. Matthews said. Her friend, the talent scout, had asked Mrs. Matthews if she knew anyone he could consider for the movies.

Julia could hardly wait to tell Henry the news. They talked together about God's call to them to be missionaries. They talked about what effect the talent scout could have on Julia's life. They prayed together. Then Julia made her decision.

"I have decided," she told Mrs. Matthews, "that I do not want to audition with the talent scout. God has called me to be a missionary. Even if the talent scout wanted me, being

in the movies is not what I must do."

"I understand, Julia," Mrs. Matthews said. She knew of Julia's plans and was not surprised at her decision.

While in high school, Henry and Julia began teaching in a mission attended by Spanish-speaking children.

Julia thought God would call her to be a missionary to Mexico. She took Spanish. She passed the tests, but she could not speak Spanish well. She did not understand why she was having such difficulty.

Henry and Julia entered Baylor University in Waco, Texas, the same year. One day during their sophomore year at Baylor, they went to chapel to hear a missionary from Persia. Henry went to his place in the chapel. Julia went to her seat. Their assigned seats were far apart.

The speaker said he was praying that God would call someone to go to Damascus to share the gospel. He explained to the students that he had stopped to spend the night in Damascus on his way home from Persia. "Thousands of Muslims in Damascus know nothing about Jesus," he said.

As Julia listened to him, she understood why she could not learn Spanish. The Lord wanted her in Damascus, Syria.

Henry and Julia met after chapel, as usual.

"Julia," Henry said excitedly, "God is calling me to serve in Syria."

Julia told him God had also called her to Syria.

Together they talked to the speaker, who told them more about the Muslim world. From that time on, Julia and Henry planned to go to Damascus.

At the end of Henry's first year in college, a church called him to be its pastor and preach one Sunday a month. Julia and Henry went home to San Antonio. First Baptist Church held a special service to ordain Henry as a preacher of the gospel.

At Baylor, Julia studied speech, drama, and English. She took the courses required for her to become an English teacher.

At Baylor she often directed plays which the Mission

Volunteer Band put on in churches in and near Waco.

On August 16, 1938, Julia and Henry were married. Their love had lasted.

For a year, she taught school in Kyle, Texas, while Henry pastored two churches, Hutto and Jarrell, both in central Texas.

In 1939, the young couple moved to Jarrell. Julia began leading churches in that area in Woman's Missionary Union work and became associational director of the work.

In January of the next year, Julia and Henry entered Southwestern Baptist Theological Seminary in Fort Worth to prepare themselves for mission work.

Every Friday, they left the campus to travel to one of their two churches, each almost two hundred miles away from the seminary. Without expressways or four-lane roads, trips took several hours. Every Monday they drove back to seminary to begin the week of classes.

Julia and Henry had little money. From the two churches, Henry received $80 a month. Julia and Henry made car payments of $30 each month. They paid $10 to rent a room across from the seminary campus. Julia cooked their meals on a hot plate. In the house where they lived they shared a bathroom with three other families.

But they were happy because they were doing what God wanted them to do.

"I have some fresh beans I grew in my garden," a church member said. "Could you use them?"

"Thank you," said Julia. "I wish I had some way to keep them fresh."

"I'll teach you how to can them," the woman volunteered. She taught Julia how to can beans, corn, peaches, and other good foods.

"Good news, Julia," Henry said one day. "The church at Frisco wants me as their full-time pastor."

That was wonderful news. Frisco was just a few miles from Fort Worth. Henry and Julia could be in the same church every week.

A Missionary Appointment

Just before Henry's seminary graduation, several students packed fried chicken, sandwiches, cookies, and fruit for picnics on a forty-eight-hour train ride. They were going from Fort Worth, Texas, to Richmond, Virginia. All were to be appointed as missionaries by the Baptist Foreign Mission Board.

"Henry and Julia Hagood, appointed for Damascus, Syria," the mission board secretary announced during the appointment service. Julia and Henry looked at each other. At last, their dream had come true.

"You have been appointed to go to a difficult place," the leader was saying. "The people in Syria are Muslims. Most of them do not want to hear about Jesus. When you come home for your first furlough, if you have not won one person to Christ, will you still be willing to go back to Syria?"

"Of course," they answered. "God has called us there." It was 1943. The world was at war. No one, except servicemen, could travel to the Middle East or anywhere else overseas. Julia and Henry would have to wait to sail to Syria. While they waited, Henry took a course in Arabic language and culture at Harvard University.

After that study, they went to Richmond, Virginia, where Henry served as pastor of Westhampton Baptist Church.

"The pastor's wife had a baby today," one church member told another one day. "His name is Jimmie. All are doing fine. The pastor is so proud of his son." The day was September 25, 1944.

Since Julia needed to be at home with her new baby, she invited the girls in her church to come to her home. She began a Girls' Auxiliary group to teach them about missions. The girls enjoyed the study, the cookies she

18

baked, and playing with the baby. Julia also trained women to serve as GA leaders, so they would be ready to take charge when she left for the mission field.

In April, 1945, the phone call they wanted came. Dr. George Sadler, the Foreign Mission Board Secretary for the Middle East, said, "I have good news. A few civilians will be allowed to go on a troopship to the Middle East. We do not know exactly where the ship will land. You can take only one piece of luggage for each of you. Can you be ready?"

"Of course," they replied. They began packing.

They needed baby food and canned milk for Jimmie. During the war, however, because of shortages, families could get only small amounts of food at one time. Julia went to the government office to get special permission to buy the food Jimmie needed.

Julia carefully packed the food into a box which she sent ahead to New York, their sailing point. But when Julia and Henry arrived in New York, they could not find the box. They had to get on the ship without food and milk for Jimmie.

"We'll just pray that Jimmie will be OK," they agreed.

Merrell and Beth Callaway, newly appointed missionaries to Beirut, Lebanon, and their child got on the same ship. Three thousand troops and two hundred civilians crowded onto the ship.

All civilian men lived in one large room. Julia, Beth, their two children, plus two other adults and two other children lived in one room. Next to them lived three women and five children.

The shower between the two rooms had water only two hours a day: 5:00-6:00 AM and 5:00-6:00 PM. Sixteen people sharing one shower created quite a problem.

In spite of the crowded conditions they were eager to get to the place where God had called them to be foreign missionaries.

One day Julia met a young sergeant who was in charge of sick bay where wounded and ill servicemen stayed. On the way to battle no one used this area. When the sergeant heard how crowded the conditions were, he arranged for the three women on board with babies to use the sick bay. There the women gave their children baths and washed diapers and other clothing. The sergeant also provided food and milk for the babies.

For weeks they sailed on the ship. One night, while the ship was in a North Africa port, the troops left the ship. In a few days, the ship landed again, and the civilians were ordered to get off. They learned they were in Port Said, Egypt. Julia, Henry, and Jimmie spent the night in a hotel.

They traveled by train to Cairo and then boarded another train for Jerusalem.

"We are finally here," Henry said to Julia. "Can you believe it? Soon we can begin our work. I'm not sure where we'll go when we get off the train."

"The Lord has cared for us until now. He will help us know what to do," commented Julia.

When the train pulled into the station in Jerusalem, they saw an American waiting for someone. They learned she was Kate Ellen Gruver, a Baptist missionary.

"I had heard that some Americans might be aboard the train," she explained. "I wanted to be here just in case you were aboard."

What a happy time for the Hagoods! While they were on the ship, World War II had ended. Peace was being restored. And the Hagoods had arrived in the Middle East. They began studying Arabic.

A Missionary Alone

Julia and Henry had agreed to work in Nazareth until more missionaries could arrive. Dr. Sadler had asked them to locate the believers who had been active in Baptist work before the war. Julia and Henry planned to get the work going again there before moving to Syria. No Baptist work had ever been done in Syria.

But no place in Nazareth could be found for them to live. The mission house was filled. So Henry had to travel from Jerusalem to Nazareth to preach on weekends.

He became ill, but he kept working. He could not seem to get his strength back. He lost fifty pounds within a few weeks.

"I think I will be OK, Julia," Henry tried to comfort worried Julia. "I needed to lose some weight. When I no longer have to ride the bus to Nazareth, and when I can eat properly, I should get better."

When Henry came back from Nazareth one weekend, he told Julia about a sick baby. Julia and Jimmie went with Henry to see about the baby. They decided to take the baby girl, named Rahdia, home with them. She was the same age as Jimmie.

On Christmas Eve, their first Christmas in the Middle East, the Hagoods went from Jerusalem to Bethlehem for a Christmas Eve service at Shepherds' Field. As they worshiped, they thought of how the shepherds must have felt as the angels announced Jesus' birth. The next day they spent Christmas in Jerusalem with their new missionary friends in the Middle East.

On December 26 they moved to Nazareth to live in the upstairs part of the mission house, next door to the Nazareth Baptist Church.

After living in Nazareth only ten days, Henry became very ill. A throat infection got so bad that he could not breathe lying down. Julia became worried. One night she did everything she could to locate a doctor, but there was no telephone. They did not have a car. The nearest telephone was in a store which was closed.

Early the next morning, as soon as the store opened, Julia called the Edinburgh Medical Mission Hospital.

A doctor came about ten o'clock. He examined Henry and told him he must get to the hospital immediately.

"He must get penicillin and lots of it," the doctor told Julia. "He needs an injection every four hours to get rid of this serious infection."

The tone of the doctor's voice told Julia she could waste no time getting Henry to the hospital. She left Jimmie and Rahdia with a maid.

The Hagoods arrived at the hospital about noon. Doctors started giving Henry penicillin.

In the hospital Henry said, "This is Saturday night. Tomorrow is Sunday. Who will be able to preach in my place?"

A young Palestinian lay preacher visiting in the hospital agreed to preach. As sick as Henry was, he did not forget the needs of the church he pastored.

Late that night, Julia was resting on a bed in Henry's room. Suddenly she sat up. She realized Henry's heavy breathing had stopped. At first she thought he must be getting better.

She called the doctor. The nurse and the doctor came quickly. They looked at Julia sadly. Henry, whom she had loved since she was fifteen, had died.

The death certificate said he died of heart failure. The doctor explained that Henry's heart could not take all the infection and was weakened from all the other illnesses he had. The infection was similar to a disease called diphtheria.

It was after midnight. As soon as she could, Julia knew she had to get back to her children. The doctor's car would not start. The doctor walked home with a heartbroken Julia.

As they walked through the narrow streets of Nazareth, the stillness of the night was broken by Jimmie's crying. While Julia and the doctor were still far away from the house, Julia heard the cries. Julia ran as fast as she could to the house, picked Jimmie up, held him close to her, and sang to him as she rocked him to sleep. He calmed down immediately.

The doctor told the woman who had been caring for Jimmie and Rahdia what had happened. The woman began to weep and wail, which is the custom in the Middle East when someone dies.

The next day people crowded into the house to comfort

24

Julia. Missionaries came. The Arab people came. Everyone who came asked, "When do you plan to leave?" or "What can I do to help you get ready to leave?"

When Julia was asked such questions, she did not know how to answer them. She had no intention of leaving. Though her husband had died, she still planned to serve God in the Middle East.

Julia felt she must leave the crowd to talk to God, though the Arabs never leave a widow alone. She locked herself in the bedroom.

"Please, God," she prayed, "give me strength to deal with my great loss. I don't know what it will be like without Henry. But I need to know one thing. What is Your will for me right now?"

At that moment Julia remembered something that had happened when she was ten years old. She was seated on the third row in the aisle seat on the lefthand side of the room in her church. She remembered hearing Mrs. Brock tell the story about David Livingstone. She remembered that, at that moment, God had called her to be a foreign missionary.

Julia thanked God for reminding her of His call. From that time on, when anyone asked her about leaving, she replied, "I am not leaving. I am staying."

Julia wondered what kind of mission work she could do in Nazareth, alone. When she thought of all the homeless babies, she found her answer. She already had little motherless Rahdia. She and Kate Ellen Gruver began a children's home. Kate Ellen took care of the business. Julia took care of the babies. People brought many babies to her.

At night, especially, when the babies were asleep, Julia felt lonely. She missed Henry very much. She could not understand why he had died when he wanted to share the gospel in Damascus.

But Julia did not have to know all the answers. She had one answer she needed: God still wanted her to be a missionary in the Middle East.

Walking and Running

"That boy should be walking," Mrs. Morrison told her daughter. "After all, Finlay is two years old."

"I know, Mother," Mrs. Graham replied. "He can get to where he wants to go faster by crawling. Walking would be too slow for him."

"We'll see," Mrs. Morrison said. She had agreed to take care of Finlay while Mrs. Graham went shopping.

"When you return," she said, "he will be walking."

And she kept her word. Mrs. Graham could hardly believe it when she returned home, and Finlay took a few shaky steps to reach her.

Once Finlay started walking, he seemed to keep a fast pace. Running became a way of life for Finlay Graham.

Kenneth Graham, Finlay's father, helped his three sons and one daughter get plenty of exercise. They worked hard. They played hard. And they walked to church at least twice on Sundays, even when they lived miles from the church. Their home was Greenock, Scotland. When they moved to the country, they walked or rode bicycles three miles each way to school.

Kenneth Graham was the son of missionaries. He always loved going to church. He led his family in worship twice every day, morning and evening, and to pray before and after every meal. Sometimes Mr. Graham preached in churches and missions when he was needed.

One summer, Finlay earned enough money by helping a salmon fisherman to buy a new racing bicycle. Now he could go faster than he could walk or run. His brother, Donnie, five years younger, tried to beat Finlay to school. Even though Donnie left earlier than his brother, Finlay always arrived at school first.

One winter morning, Finlay whizzed past Donnie. As he went around a corner, his bicycle skidded on an icy patch. Though he was unhurt, he ripped his pants. A friend with safety pins came to the rescue. But Finlay had to face his mother that evening.

"Finlay, Finlay, why do you always have to go so fast? Why do you always have to be first in every race?" his mother asked. "Now let's talk about how you must be punished."

To Finlay, his mother's disapproval was punishment enough. But his mother always had other ideas about punishment.

Finlay played all kinds of sports. He wanted to play every game in every sport. And he always wanted to win. Once he was determined to play a game, even though he had a chest cold. His team won, but he became seriously ill with pneumonia.

There were no antibiotics in the early 1900s. Because no drugs could help in his cure, fear grew that the pneumonia would take his life. High fever, pain, and discomfort filled his days.

One day the doctor came to Finlay's room, examined him again, and said to his parents, "I can do no more for your son. He may not live until tomorrow. If he gets through the crisis, he will get well."

Mr. and Mrs. Graham knelt and prayed that God would save Finlay's life. The next day Finlay began to get better. He soon was running and playing again.

Summer with Grandparents

The Graham boys liked to spend summer vacations with their grandparents on the little island of Scalpay, Harris, off the west coast of Scotland. One summer, Finlay and his brother, John, went together. The brothers traveled by boat for two-and-one-half days to get from their home in Greenock to their grandparents' home. Their mother packed enough food to last them during the trip.

The boys loved to go on fishing trips with their grandfather. They would go out at night and cast their nets. The next morning they hauled in the fish caught in the nets overnight.

One evening they were fishing with their grandfather and his crew near the coast in the west of Scotland.

"Get down the Book," Grandfather Morrison said. Finlay and John knew exactly what he meant. He wanted the Bible.

As the sun was setting, the fishing crew heard strains of music coming across the ocean to their boat. As they listened, they realized that some fishermen in another boat were also worshiping together.

Grandfather Morrison did lobster and herring fishing. He also had a small farm with sheep, a milk cow, and chickens. The boys liked to watch Grandmother Morrison weave the wool taken from their sheep, card it, and make the famous Harris tweed material.

Finlay liked to take things apart and put them back together. The only problem was that sometimes he could not get them back together the way that they were before.

Once Finlay repaired a clock. Later, his mother found a part, a spring, that was left over. She knew the clock would not run without a spring. Yet the clock was running. When she inspected the clock, she found that the spring had been replaced with a rubber band.

Scrubbing the kitchen floor, one of Finlay's jobs, was his least favorite. But he did it—as fast as he could do it well.

He liked going outdoors with his dad to cut firewood. Coal cost so much that the family could buy a sack only once every month or two.

Finlay and his dad cut the branches from a tree. Then they carried the log home to cut up for firewood. Finlay carried the light end, in front. His dad took the heavy end, at the back.

One time, Finlay felt that his end of the log was much lighter than it should be. He looked back. His dad was carrying the middle, making Finlay's load especially light.

The country school Finlay attended had thirty children in six elementary grades in one room. The school had no piped-in water and no bathroom.

When children became thirsty, they went outside to a stream where they cupped water in their hands.

"Finlay, it is time to come in," his teacher had to remind him more than once. He would become so interested in watching the brown trout in the stream that he forgot all about school.

The teacher taught the Bible to the schoolchildren. The minister in the town came often to check on what the children had learned. Finlay memorized whole chapters of the Bible.

In the one-room school, the younger children sat at the front, with the others toward the back. Miss MacQuarrie, the teacher, taught all six grades. The younger children could hear her teach the older children. By the time Finlay got to the sixth grade, he had already learned much of what she taught to sixth graders. He had heard it many times before.

"Your son is the best in my class this year," the teacher told the Grahams. And that was true each year for Finlay. He loved all subjects, especially math. As he studied algebra, geometry, and calculus, he wanted to learn all he could. He even studied six years of Latin before he graduated from high school.

One day Finlay decided to set a match to some dry grass on a hillside. He had watched others burn off the grass. He wanted to help. He was alone.

The wind began to blow. The fire began to spread. Finlay was afraid he would set the whole hillside on fire. He found an old can, filled it with water, and rushed back and forth to pour water on the fire. Finally, he had the fire out.

Again, he had to go home to his mother. His clothes were dirty. He could not hide this mistake from his mother. Again, he displeased her.

"I am sorry, Mother," was all he could say.

He Played to Win

The older Finlay got, the more he enjoyed sports. He wanted to win every game he played. Once when playing hounds and hare, as the hare he ran so fast to get back to safety that he ran straight into another boy.

"Watch out, Finlay," a friend called.

But it was too late. About that time, Finlay crashed head-on with another runner coming around the corner of the schoolhouse. His nose hit the other boy's forehead. One of his nostrils remained partially blocked because of that collision.

Finlay liked to play rounders, a game like baseball. He also liked soccer, running, and shinny, a game like field hockey. Though the teams had no coaches, his father encouraged him to play. Finlay could not afford soccer shoes and had to play barefoot in soccer games.

The Grahams lived near the sea in Scotland. Finlay learned to row while salmon fishing in a heavy boat. When he was seventeen, he entered a boat race called a regatta. The boats in the race were much lighter than the fishing boats.

"You cannot win, Finlay," his father predicted. "Everyone else in the race is a full-grown man. You don't weigh enough. You have not had enough experience."

But Finlay always liked a challenge. When the race was over, he had won easily, two lengths ahead of the second boat.

One time Mr. Graham worked as manager of an estate. On the estate were several fruit trees. One day Finlay picked some plums from a tree.

He was enjoying the plums when suddenly Mr. McDonald, the owner of the estate, caught him.

"Finlay, what are you doing here?" he asked.

"If you tell my father what I did, it will break his heart," Finlay confessed. "If you will not tell him, I promise I will never take anything from anyone else's tree again."

Both kept their promise.

One Sunday afternoon Finlay, his older brother, John, and a friend attended a special service for children. Two missionary women were holding services in the village.

Finlay listened intently as the missionary explained clearly how to become a Christian.

At the end of the service, the missionary said, "I invite you to accept Christ as your Lord and Savior."

Finlay wanted to go tell the missionary that he wanted to become a Christian. But he looked at his brother. He looked at his friend. Neither one seemed interested in what was happening. Though Finlay wanted to become a Christian, that day he did not make that decision.

When Finlay was fifteen, his mother became very ill. She had to go to Glasgow for a serious operation.

"Please, God, bring her home safely," he prayed. "If You will make her well, I will give my life to You."

His mother came home from the hospital. Soon she was well. But Finlay did not keep his promise.

After high school, Finlay went away to the University of Glasgow. One day he received a telegram.

"Come home. Dad seriously ill," was all it said.

When Finlay got home, he learned what had happened. On the way home from a deacons' meeting, Mr. Graham had been struck down by a drunken driver on his way to a dance. But the driver did not stop to help him. Later a woman found him and took him to a hospital.

Finlay rushed to the hospital to see his dad. He began to pray, "Lord, if You will save my dad's life, I will live for You."

His dad recovered. But Finlay did not keep his promise.

One Monday afternoon, Finlay and some friends were standing outside the university gates. He had been friends since high school with some of these boys. The group of students began telling jokes, some of them dirty.

Finlay joined in the fun. He began telling jokes. His friends were laughing.

All of a sudden, Finlay quit talking. He began thinking about what he was doing. He knew he was wrong to be telling such jokes.

Quickly, he excused himself from his friends. He began to run. He ran and ran and ran. Finally, he could run no farther. He began to pray, "Lord, save me."

When he got to his room, he knelt by his bed. He opened his Bible to 1 John 1:9. He read, "If we confess our sins, he is faithful and just to forgive us our sins, and to cleanse us from all unrighteousness."

At that moment, he gave his life to God.

One day Finlay read again the story of David Livingstone, the missionary. He had read the story first in one of the few books his parents had. As he prayed, he thought about that story. God used this story to help Finlay understand the needs of persons in the world who had not heard the gospel. As he kept praying, Finlay began to know that God wanted him to be a foreign missionary.

Finding God's Will

At first, Finlay told no one he had become a Christian. He did write to his parents. The letter his mother wrote in return brought tears to his eyes.

"I always prayed extra hard for you, Finlay. You do everything in such an intense way that I feared what would happen to you. Now all of your energy and enthusiasm can and will be used to spread the gospel. I am praying for you."

Finlay joined the Christian Students Fellowship in Glasgow. Each Sunday afternoon, the students conducted outside services. They went to an intersection where hundreds of people passed by. Persons walking by would stop a minute, listen to the message, and then move on.

"I have an idea," one student said. "Let's have several groups, one at each intersection. That way, people will hear more of the gospel message. If they stop a minute each time, they will hear something at every corner."

The students tried it. Sure enough, they realized that people would hear some of the message even if they never stopped walking.

Finlay decided to read the Bible through. Within six months of becoming a Christian, he had done it. During his reading, he became convinced of two things. First, he believed that the Bible teaches everyone to give at least a tenth of his income to the Lord.

Second, he believed that baptism is by immersion only and that every Christian should follow God's command and example by being baptized. For these reasons, Finlay Graham decided to become a Baptist.

Finlay could hardly wait to become a missionary. But he knew he had to prepare first. He wanted to enter medical school right away because he believed at the time he should become a medical missionary.

He decided to ask the director of the missions society for advice. The director told him, "The first thing you must do is to finish your work at the university, Finlay. After that, you can probably get a scholarship to go to Edinburgh for your medical training."

Finlay took that advice. He went back to Glasgow to finish his studies. But the war which became known as World War II was declared September 3, 1939.

"What should I do?" Finlay prayed. "I want to finish school, but my country needs me too."

Finlay volunteered to fly in the Royal Air Force. He wanted to be a pilot.

"We need you as a navigator because you are good at math," the officer in charge told him.

Finlay accepted this assignment. But he decided to delay his service until he graduated from the University of Glasgow.

After his graduation, Finlay entered the Royal Air Force to begin navigation training.

During World War II, Finlay flew to thirty different countries. Twice he was almost killed. Once his plane crashed into the sea.

Once two German naval vessels were escorting an ammunition ship in the Aegean Sea. Finlay's plane flew low to torpedo the ammunition ship. The two escort vessels opened fire on his plane.

Finlay stood close to the escape hatch. He hoped to get into a lifeboat when the plane went down. But the plane did not crash. He was safe.

While he was in training in England, he sometimes received a weekend pass to go home to Scotland. He would not tell his parents when he was coming.

As he arrived home each time, his mother would say, "I expected you today. I dreamed of you last night. And the Lord brought you home."

In the Royal Air Force, as Finlay flew over country after country, he would ask the Lord, "Is this the country where you want me to serve?"

For a year he taught navigators who were waiting in Jerusalem to receive their assignments.

One day a missionary in Jerusalem said to him, "You love the Arabic people. They respond to you. They love you. Perhaps the Lord is calling you here."

Finlay was unsure. He spent a weekend in prayer and fasting, asking God to tell him where He wanted him to be a missionary.

He went to the garden tomb where many believe Jesus was laid after He died on the cross. Finlay began to pray.

"Lord, if you would like to tell me where you want me to serve, I am ready. I will obey."

As he left that place of prayer, he knew God's answer. God wanted him to serve the Arabic-speaking people in the Middle East.

After serving in the Royal Air Force for six years, Finlay at last went back home to Scotland.

How excited Mrs. Graham was to have her son back

home. He told his mother that he would have to leave soon to go to Jerusalem to study the Arabic language.

"Son, how will you finance your missionary travels? Have you thought about that?" his mother asked.

Finlay knew he needed some money. But he did not know where he would get it. He applied to a travel agent to go by sea to Palestine. He waited and waited. Finally he learned he had passage on a ship to Palestine. But he still had no money. He knew that God would help him find a way.

When he told his mother that he had been cleared for passage to Palestine, she took from her purse a postal savings book. She showed it to Finlay.

"Mother, where did you get this money?" Finlay asked.

"For six years, Son, you have been sending me two thirds of your salary in the Royal Air Force. I have placed every penny of it in savings. This is your money. Use it now to do what God wants you to do."

All this time, Finlay had planned for his parents to use that money for themselves. But his mother was planning to make it easier for him to continue to follow God's will.

He thanked his mother over and over. Finlay thanked God that He had provided for his needs long before Finlay even knew he would need money for a long trip. He boarded the ship that would take him to a new life as a missionary in the Middle East.

Two Students Meet

"I must spend some time concentrating on the study of the language," Julia told the other missionaries.

"There is a course in Jerusalem," one friend told her. "Let's work out our mission work schedule so you can go for the three months' spring term."

Julia and Jimmie moved to Jerusalem. She enrolled in the beginning Arabic class, but it was too easy. After all, she had been with Arabic-speaking people for almost two years. She could speak the language some, but she wanted to read it and understand it better.

After a week, she moved to the advanced class. The three people in that class had been studying together every day for six months.

"How will I ever catch up in this class?" she wondered as she studied.

"I'll be glad to come to your place this afternoon to help you with your Arabic, if you like," a man in the class said.

That young Scotsman was Finlay Graham.

When Finlay arrived at the hostel (a kind of boarding house) that afternoon, Julia and Finlay began their study. Soon Jimmie woke up from his afternoon nap and joined the two grown-ups. He looked at the strange man. He looked at his mother. Then he climbed into Finlay's lap and sat there for the whole lesson.

Every afternoon Finlay and Julia studied. Jimmie played with his toys or sat on Finlay's lap.

Jimmie liked his mother's new friend. He went everywhere with them. In Arab countries, couples do not date. Finlay, Julia, and Jimmie went often to the Jewish section of the city. No one there paid much attention to the young couple and the small boy. Julia and Finlay walked and talked. They bought ice cream. They began to feel that it was God's will for them to marry. By this time, they loved each other very much.

They talked to the other Baptist missionaries to tell them of their plans to marry. The missionaries wrote to the Foreign Mission Board to say they felt Finlay should be appointed as a Southern Baptist missionary.

In July the Baptist World Alliance met in Copenhagen, Denmark. Finlay went to the meeting to talk to officials from the Foreign Mission Board. He asked them to appoint him as a missionary.

"We will let you know after the Board meets," he was told.

Finlay and Julia planned to be married even before they knew the Board's decision.

Julia's mother, now living in Fort Worth, Texas, received a letter from her excited daughter: "Finlay and I are getting married. Can you come?"

Mrs. Saccar wasted no time. Julia had sent her mother a magazine picture of a suit she liked. Her mother bought the pattern and fabric. She also bought other clothing that Julia and Finlay needed. She made her plans to go to Nazareth for the wedding.

Mrs. Saccar had trouble getting to the wedding on time. There were no passenger ships and she had to ride on a cargo ship. She arrived just two days before the wedding. Mother and daughter worked hard to get the wedding dress made in time.

After the wedding, the newly married couple began walking up the aisle. Jimmie slipped away from his grandmother and grabbed the hands of the newlyweds. He did not want them to leave without him.

Julia and Finlay took a short trip that included two days in Damascus where Julia and Henry had wanted to serve.

The couple returned to Nazareth by bus. They walked by the post office on their way to the mission house. A telegram from the Foreign Mission Board said that Finlay had been appointed as a Southern Baptist missionary.

The date on the telegram, September 11, was the same as their wedding date. They felt happy that God had made it possible for both of them to serve together as missionaries in the Middle East.

The Board assigned the Grahams to begin work in Jordan. But they could not get visas (permits) to go there. After they went to Jerusalem to ask help from the American Embassy, they received their visas with much difficulty.

On the way back from Jerusalem to Nazareth, they stopped in Nablus to ask directions to a friend's house. Suddenly, a mob of people surrounded the station wagon which Finlay was driving.

"Shall we kill them here or take them somewhere else?" they heard a man say. All the men in charge carried guns.

They decided to take the Grahams to the mayor of the town to get his decision.

Two men with guns sat on the car. Two other men with guns crawled into the back seat with Jimmie and Mrs. Saccar. The men inside the car gave Finlay orders, telling him where to drive.

A Palestinian Arab with a British accent came outside to talk to the Grahams when they arrived at a building. The man asked Finlay to explain what they were doing in the town. Finlay did.

"I believe you," he said. "You were stopped because we had word that spies were coming in a station wagon."

The Grahams went on to Nazareth without stopping.

The Jews and the Arabs in the Middle East were at war. Many times the missionaries narrowly escaped serious harm or death.

Late one night, Jameel, their friend, knocked on their door.

"Tonight there was a mass meeting in the town square," he said excitedly. "They decided that you are here to store arms for the enemy. Three persons are coming tomorrow to kill you. You must leave now!"

"We are not leaving," the Grahams said.

The next day, the three men came. The Grahams invited them in. Julia served them Arabic coffee and sweets.

"Since this is your first time to visit us," said Julia, "perhaps you would like to see the house."

As she led them from one room to another, she opened all the cupboards and every closet. The men could see easily that no arms were being stored in the house. Inside the cupboards were baby diapers, baby clothes, and food for the Baptist children's home.

As the men left, they thanked the Grahams for the good work they were doing for their people.

Moving to Jordan

"Where are we going to live and begin our work in Jordan?" the Grahams asked. No Baptists had ever worked in Jordan before.

They decided on a plan. In each village they visited they would tell the people why they wanted to come. They would ask for a place to rent. When they found a place to rent, they would know that God wanted them to start work in that village.

"I'll rent you a house," a man in Taibe said.

"We'll take it," the Grahams said.

Before the family moved, Finlay worked hard to repair the house. He put glass and screens on the windows. He built an outside bathroom.

Taibe had no running water, no electricity, no phones, no doctor, no drug store, only an open-air vegetable and meat market. Over 6,000 people lived in the village. Only one man could speak English. The Grahams had to speak Arabic to the people in Taibe. Julia was glad she had studied hard!

Before the water in Taibe could be used, Julia strained it through a filter to take out the impurities. Then she boiled the water before she could use it.

Julia noticed that the children in Taibe had all kinds of diseases. Most of them had infected eyes. She wanted to help. Soon there were forty to fifty children coming to her house three times a day to get Julia to wash out their eyes with boric acid or strong tea.

Then people began to come with other illnesses. Though Julia was not a doctor or a nurse, she knew that cleanliness would help heal some of the diseases.

The people wanted to say thank you. They brought the

Grahams whatever they could—olives and other gifts.

Finlay preached, and Julia played their portable pump organ in the Sunday services. They tried to teach the Arabic people to sing. During the services people came in when they wanted and left when they got ready.

"How many times did you begin your sermon today, Finlay?" Julia teased.

"Probably two or three times," he replied seriously. "How can I preach a whole sermon when people come in and leave at different times during the service?"

People began asking questions about Jesus. But no one became a Christian. At least, that is what the Grahams thought.

In Beirut, Lebanon, half a day's drive away, several people were meeting for worship. Finlay visited there. The people in Beirut asked Finlay and Julia to come there to teach them about Jesus.

The Grahams said no. They felt God was leading them to stay in Taibe.

The next time Finlay came back from a visit to Beirut, he asked Julia, "Do you think the Lord wants us to move to Beirut?"

"No, I don't. We have work to do here," Julia said.

"I agree with you. But the people in Beirut seem convinced that God wants us there."

"Well, I will pray about it," Julia said, "but we need to stay in Taibe."

After she prayed, she felt strongly that they should go to Beirut, but only to visit.

When they arrived for a visit, a woman said, "We have been expecting you. I will take you to see the house."

The Grahams had no idea what house she was talking about.

"A group of us have been praying for three days and nights that you would come to live and work here. At the end of the third day, we felt that God was leading you to help us. Were we wrong?"

As Julia listened, she realized that the third day the people in Beirut were praying was the same day that she had felt God leading them to visit Beirut.

The woman continued with her story.

"As soon as I knew that God was leading you here, I began praying. I knew you would need a house and a place to hold services. One day I was praying while I was washing dishes. My son came in and asked me to go to a house where they were selling a table he needed for his work.

"When I went to see the table, I went inside and saw a large central room with other rooms around it. I knew this house would be the perfect place for you. And the house was for rent. I thanked God. I have made arrangements for you to see the house."

Julia and Finlay could hardly believe what they were hearing. They went to the house and agreed it was a perfect place to live and to hold services.

"I feel I should rent this house to you," the woman in the house said. "Others have come wanting to rent the house, but it is yours if you want it."

Julia and Finlay decided that God must be leading them to Beirut.

But there was a big problem. Rent had to be paid a year in advance. The Grahams borrowed money to hold the house until they could ask the Foreign Mission Board about it.

They wrote a letter asking to be transferred from Jordan to Beirut. They asked for money to rent the house. A month later the answer came.

The Grahams were to serve in Beirut. Finlay went to Taibe to load their household goods to move to Beirut, Lebanon. On Thanksgiving Day, 1948, the Grahams moved to the house in Beirut.

The Happiest Years

People crowded into the large house in Beirut. Sunday School classes met in every room. Finlay led services almost every evening. The Lebanese people came day and night to visit Julia and Finlay. The Grahams welcomed each one. Many people became Christians.

Julia began holding meetings for women and children. Six women came to the first missions meeting. They prayed aloud before others for the first time in their lives. They prayed for missionaries throughout the world. They studied the Bible.

Julia needed study material in the Arabic language for these missions meetings. She used her daily Arabic lesson to translate material from magazines in English.

Julia and Finlay stayed especially busy on Sundays. They led morning services in Beirut. In the afternoons Finlay took one group of people to a village for Sunday School and preaching services. Another group crowded into the station wagon with Julia and the pump organ to go to lead Sunday School and worship in another area.

The time finally came when the Grahams could go home on furlough. For five years, they had worked as missionaries. Now they could go home to Scotland and then the United States.

"I can hardly believe it," Finlay said. "At last my parents can meet my wife."

"You have told me so much about them that I can hardly wait," said Julia. "We can have a good visit with them. Then we can go to my home, and you can meet my friends."

After visiting Finlay's home, the couple traveled to Fort Worth, Texas. Finlay spent the time studying at Southwestern Baptist Theological Seminary. Their first daughter,

Catherine, was born while they were living in Fort Worth.

When they returned to Beirut, the mission work kept growing. Finlay preached somewhere every night. Other missionaries began arriving to help.

Missionary Anna Cowan came to Lebanon for a year of Arabic study before moving to Jordan. Though she had planned to leave the United States on July 2, a last-minute change in plans meant she had to leave June 2. She sailed without knowing the name of anyone in Beirut.

As her ship arrived early in the morning of June 23, little boats came out to the ship to take passengers to the dock. Anna had no idea where she would go.

As she stood on the deck awaiting her turn on the rope ladder to the little boat, she heard someone call her name.

"Anna, Anna Cowan." A man was standing up in one of the small boats waving his hand and calling.

Soon Finlay Graham was on board to help her. He helped her through customs and took her to his home. Julia had cooked a wonderful meal.

Another time, the Grahams helped some servicemen who were new Christians. They often shared their home in this way.

Commander Cravens, a Baptist US Navy chaplain, visited the Grahams in Beirut during the spring of 1956.

"I have some men ready to be baptized," he said. Their carrier, the *Coral Sea*, was anchored in port at Beirut.

Just in front of the mission house was a water storage tank used for a building project. The chaplain could baptize there.

For the baptismal service, neighbors gathered on rooftops and balconies of buildings in order to be high enough to see the baptism in the storage tank. Before the baptismal service, the chaplain preached in English. Finlay translated into Arabic. Though there was no public address system, none was needed.

Finlay's powerful voice was heard even a half block away. Then the chaplain baptized the servicemen in the water tank.

As the work grew, many new Arab Christians began

leading services in other areas around Beirut.

"These men need to be trained as pastors and preachers," Finlay said. For three days each week Finlay taught them. Julia met with the women to teach them how to read the Bible. She helped some young people learn to play the piano to help in the worship services.

By 1956 the missionaries had led in completing three buildings—a house for three missionary families, a school, and a church building.

At first only four-year-olds came to school. Kindergarten and grade school came next. Each year a new grade was added. In the school Finlay taught Bible to high school classes. Julia taught a high school English class for several years.

In the first graduating class of the Beirut Baptist School, all but three graduates had become Christians. Julia had taught them English for four years. Finlay had taught them Bible in Arabic.

Later, a student who had moved to Vienna, Austria, came back to Beirut. She said to the Grahams, "I want to tell you I am a real Christian." She was one of the three who had graduated before becoming a Christian.

At last, the Lottie Moon Christmas Offering made it possible for Southern Baptists to buy property for a seminary—a school to train persons who wanted to become pastors and leaders in churches.

In October 1961, the seminary opened on the new campus. For the first time as missionaries, the Grahams could stay in one place to do their work. They did not need to travel from place to place to share the gospel.

Instead, the students came to them for training. Finlay taught the young people how to study the Bible and how to preach.

Julia taught English. Since few textbooks were written in Arabic, she wanted the students to be able to read the books in English. She also taught drama to each class of students. She taught wives of students how they could work in churches with their husbands.

The civil war in Lebanon, which began in 1975,

51

sometimes made it difficult to do missions work. Much shooting and killing took place. Some missionaries were even kidnapped. From day to day, the missionaries never knew what to expect.

One day, two seminary students called Finlay at his home. They had returned from Jordan where they had spent their Easter break from studies.

"We cannot get back to the seminary," they told Finlay. "There is fighting on the road."

Finlay got into his car and started after them. Crowds of people were on the road. Someone tried to stop the car. Finlay drove on, though bullets shattered on the road in front of the car. He picked up the students and started back to the seminary.

A group of men with guns stopped the car. They took Finlay and the students to their secret headquarters. They searched the car and found some tracts in the glove compartment.

One tract was called "Faith Dispels Fear."

Finlay spoke to the man who had the tract in his hand, "If you are interested in the faith that dispels fear, come to my home, and I will tell you more."

The man turned to his friends. "I think we have the wrong man here. He is a preacher of the gospel and does not mean any harm."

Ten minutes later, Finlay and the students were back home at the seminary.

For sixteen years, the Grahams worked at the seminary. Finlay served as president. Now students taught at the seminary are serving as pastors of churches and in other ways throughout the Middle East.

Physically Fit

The Jim Raglands, new missionaries, had just arrived in Beirut. Ten days on a ship on a stormy sea had left them exhausted.

When Finlay met the Raglands, he grabbed a heavy trunk in each hand and told Jim to do the same. Finlay, trunks in hand, went up the steps, two at a time. Jim stood watching in amazement at Finlay's physical strength.

Everyone who knows Finlay Graham knows how important it is to him to be physically fit. He wants to be able to do whatever God leads him to do.

At one time, Finlay was getting up at five o'clock every morning and going to bed about midnight each night. He had so much he wanted to do that it was hard for him to slow down.

Once some missionaries at the seminary needed a translator for a seminary textbook. They needed someone who knew Arabic and understood theology well enough to translate the book. The missionaries asked Finlay to do it.

Finlay explained his schedule and told them he could not do it. "You must find someone else," he suggested. The missionaries could not find anyone else to do it. They went back to Finlay.

"Then I'll get up at four o'clock each morning in order to do it," he said. He did. The book was translated, published, and is used by students at the seminary in Beirut. Finlay set a goal of preparing in Arabic one textbook for the seminary each year.

Wherever the Grahams go, Finlay joins any game he sees. During his first year in Beirut, some American friends had a July 4 picnic in the mountains. They began playing baseball. Finlay had never seen a baseball game.

He did not know the rules. But he wanted to play.

His team was at bat first. He was the first one in line to bat. He picked up the bat. He hit the first ball that came to him. The ball went so far that it was easily a home run. But Finlay just stood there.

Julia began hollering to him, "Run, Finlay, run."

"Where shall I run?" he asked. When he was told where to run, he still had time to make a home run before the ball was thrown back.

Finlay always had played hard and well. No one was surprised that he hit a home run the first time he was ever up to bat!

One evening just before dusk, Finlay decided to jog before supper. When he crossed the highway, the driver of a car did not see him. The force of the impact knocked Finlay onto the hood of the car and his head crashed through the windshield. Someone took Finlay home.

As Finlay walked into the kitchen where Julia was, she realized that he was hurt badly and needed medical help.

When they arrived at the hospital, Finlay fainted. The doctor took X rays of his skull. He feared Finlay had a concussion or worse injuries. Finlay spent the night in the hospital.

The next day the doctor showed Finlay the X rays.

"This is the thickest skull I have ever seen in an X ray," the doctor told him.

From that day on, others kidded Finlay about his "thick skull." Finlay went home the day after his accident.

Those who saw the small car which hit him said it looked as if a truck had hit it because of the heavy damage the collision caused.

The next year, in March 1967, another accident happened as Finlay drove from his home at the seminary down to a deacons' meeting in Beirut one Sunday afternoon. It was raining. A storm had knocked out the electricity.

The car skidded. It hit a large concrete foundation for an electric pylon. The impact threw Finlay unconscious to the passenger side of the car. The driver's side crashed into the concrete foundation.

Electric wires fell on the car. Those trying to help Finlay could not touch him for fear of electrocution. Firemen came and freed Finlay, still unconscious, from the wrecked car.

When Finlay was brought to the government hospital, no one there knew him. The hospital staff refused to treat him but searched his pockets to find a phone number. Finally someone located Julia. Friends took her to the hospital.

On the way there, Julia saw Finlay's car, badly damaged. She felt sure, from looking at the car, that Finlay was so badly injured that he could not live a normal life. She began to pray.

Inside the hospital, she saw Finlay lying on a stretcher in the hallway. The doctors refused treatment until they were sure someone would pay.

Church people filled the hallways. Missionary Jim Ragland talked to the doctor.

"If you know how to pray, you had better do it," the doctor advised. As Jim bent over the stretcher to talk to Finlay, he realized how seriously injured Finlay was.

Finlay, returning to consciousness briefly, opened his eyes. "Jim, I have to get to the church. I'm to preach in the evening service."

"Other arrangements will be made," Jim assured him. Finlay had broken ribs, a crushed kidney, a collapsed lung, and a broken leg. He asked to be taken to another hospital where his doctor friend worked.

But the government owned all the ambulances. The officials said the ambulances could not be used to transfer patients from one hospital to another.

A man who was a new Christian volunteered to help. His job was to repair damage done to the ambulances.

"I'll take one of those ambulances," he said to those in charge. And he did. He used it to transport Finlay to another hospital and then took the ambulance back.

Even though several ribs were broken, Finlay's muscles were so strong, and his body so fit, that the muscles held the ribs in place while they healed.

In a few weeks, Finlay went back to his work.

In Beirut, three daughters—Rose Mary, Christine, and Sheila—were born to Finlay and Julia. With Jimmie and Catherine, they now had five children. The Graham family set a good example for others as they worshiped and played together.

The Grahams enforced several rules at home. The children had to obey. They could not tell lies. They had to use Sundays for worship and serving God.

One day Jimmie came home from school, excited that he had been chosen to play on a ball team.

"When is the first game?" his father asked.

"Sunday morning at 10:30," Jimmie replied.

"I will be preaching in the Baptist church in Beirut then," Finlay said. "What shall I say when people ask where you are?"

"I won't play on Sunday," Jimmie answered.

He called the coach to tell him his decision. When the coach said, "I'll see you next Sunday," Jimmie explained, "I won't play any Sunday." The coach told him he could not be on the team.

"The will of God is not always easy," the Grahams told Jimmie, "but it is always best."

Jimmie trained hard as an athlete. Finlay helped him train for track. When Finlay picked him up after school, he would stop a mile from home so that Jimmie could run the last mile, up a steep hill.

When the two ran together, Finlay never let Jimmie beat him until he could do it honestly.

In a track meet at the American school, Jimmie once earned four first-place ribbons. He won the 100-meter, the 60-meter dash, and the shotput, and was anchorman on the winning relay team.

When one of the Graham children did well, Finlay always challenged them to do better.

The summer of 1975 was a happy, busy time for the Grahams. Three of their daughters—Catherine, Christine, and Sheila—were all married that summer. Jimmie had married in 1964, and Rose Mary in 1972. All except Catherine married while in college.

The Grahams received permission from the Foreign Mission Board to go to their daughters' three weddings. Julia made the wedding dresses for all her daughters, including Rose Mary.

All of the children, married and with families, now live in Texas, except for Sheila, who is serving with her husband and family as a missionary in Africa.

Two New Jobs

"Will you be the associate director for the Middle East?" Dr. John Hughey, director, asked Finlay.

This job meant Finlay would travel to all the countries in the Middle East. He would visit missionaries. He would preach in churches and lead conferences in many countries.

The Grahams took the job. At first, they lived in Beirut. But war restrictions meant that they could not travel directly from Lebanon to Israel. Instead, they had to fly from Beirut to a neutral country—one that was not involved in the war—and fly from there to Israel.

In 1977, the Grahams moved to Cyprus, a neutral country. From there, they could go to any other country.

In the new job Julia had to do secretarial work, which she did not enjoy. But no one else could do it. No other missionaries lived in Cyprus.

Finlay traveled almost all the time. Sometimes Julia went with him. As they visited the various countries, the Grahams became friends with all the Southern Baptist missionaries in the Middle East.

In the new job, the Grahams helped direct missionary work in Egypt, Israel, Gaza, Jordan, Lebanon, Libya, Morocco, and Yemen. By 1984, there were 162 missionaries serving those areas. Thirty-eight churches, two hospitals, the seminary in Beirut, Baptist publications, and a broadcasting ministry helped to reach persons for the gospel.

Finlay flew from one country to another to preach or to speak. When he preached in a revival in Haifa, Israel, twenty persons became Christians. Finlay gave the commencement address in the Nazareth Baptist School. He led a revival in Irbid, Jordan. He encouraged missionaries in their work.

Constant fighting in the Middle East made mission work more difficult. In February 1984, several missionary families had to be evacuated from war-torn Lebanon. Yet many persons became Christians and were baptized in 1984, and missionaries established five new preaching points.

In 1984, the Beirut Baptist School had to extend classes for two months because of time lost due to fighting. But more than 800 students were enrolled in the school.

The missionaries and the Arabs welcomed Julia and Finlay every time they came. They enjoyed working together to spread the gospel in the Middle East.

"We must know the language. We must learn the customs. We must love the people," the Grahams often reminded themselves and the other missionaries.

"One thing still concerns me," said Finlay. "The Arabs need more books in their language. Someone needs to write a church history book. Some of the seminary courses still have no Arabic textbooks."

"Could it be, Finlay," asked Julia, "that the Lord is leading us to do this translation and publication work? We have been here for forty years. It seems to me we know as much about the language as anyone else."

Finlay and Julia prayed to know God's will. Finlay decided to resign his work as associate director for the Middle East. He spent the last months before retirement translating and writing in the Arabic language.

During this time, the Grahams often went to services where children and grandchildren of persons who became Christians under their ministry were being baptized.

After Julia had spoken to the annual women's missionary meeting in Jordan one time, a middle-aged woman came up

to her. "Do you know me?" she asked.

Julia said, "I do not remember your name. I am sorry."

"I am Asma," the woman said.

Quickly Julia remembered the early years in the village of Taibe. She had thought no one had become a Christian while the Grahams were there.

A twelve-year-old girl had helped with the housework in their home in Taibe in 1948. Her name was Asma. Julia had not seen her for over thirty years! Asma told her she was married and active in women's missionary work.

After another meeting in Jordan, a man came to Finlay and called him his "father in the faith." Finlay did not know what he meant. Then he told Finlay that he had been stationed in Taibe while he was in the army. He talked with Finlay after a meeting and became a Christian after their conversation together. Now, years later, this man was leading Christian work in another place.

Remember

Julia Graham shares these ideas for boys and girls who read this book:

"The Lord helps those who help themselves. The Lord gives us the ability to think, to choose, and to work in ways that are pleasing to Him."

"Be dependable. You might not be beautiful or talented, and you cannot help it if you are not, but you can do what you say you will do."

"No life is more wonderful than a life spent in the will of God, seeking to serve Him and to follow His leadership. I just wish I had another life to give to the Middle East."

Look through this book to find ways that dependable Julia used her abilities to follow God's will for her life.

Finlay shares these ideas for readers of this book:

"Diligence is important. The best ability is availability. When we make ourselves available to God, He will certainly use us for His glory."

"I have two main goals in life. First of all, to get as many people as possible to read the Bible and to spend time in prayer. My second ambition is to get as many people as possible engaged in jogging or some other beneficial physical exercise."

"The will of God is not always easy. But the will of God is always best. My guide for living is this: seek, find, and do God's will. God has a perfect plan for every one of us. His plan is that we should be saved and then commit our lives completely to Him."

Find events in Finlay's life that demonstrate ways that he has followed God's will in his life.

About the Author

Whether serving in the education ministry of a church or ministering to students on a college campus, I have spent part of each year since my college graduation writing for children. I am grateful for the special privilege of writing this story about a missionary couple whom I have not met, but who have shared with me on tape and on paper the wonderful story of God's leadership throughout their lives. My life has been changed by this couple's story. I hope yours will be, too, as you read this story.